A GIFT FOR:

_____

FROM:

_____

© Copyright 2017 Hallmark Licensing, LLC

Published by Hallmark Gift Books,
a division of Hallmark Cards, Inc.,
Kansas City, MO 64141
Visit us on the Web at Hallmark.com.

All rights reserved. No part of this publication may be reproduced, transmitted, or stored in any form or by any means without the prior written permission of the publisher.

Editorial Director: Theresa Trinder
Editor: Kara Goodier
Art Director: Chris Opheim
Designer: Brian Pilachowski
Production Designer: Dan Horton

ISBN: 978-1-63059-772-6
BOK1067

Made in China
0621

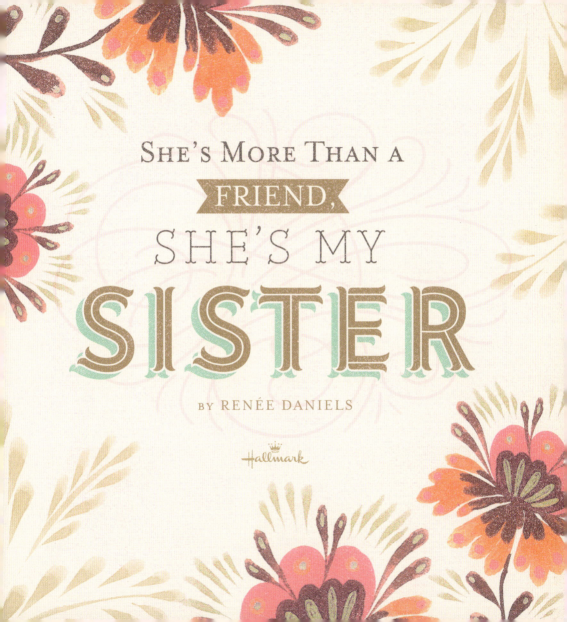

My
SISTER
IS MY
FRIEND
FOR SO MANY
DIFFERENT REASONS—

MORE SO THAN
SHE'S
PROBABLY
AWARE.

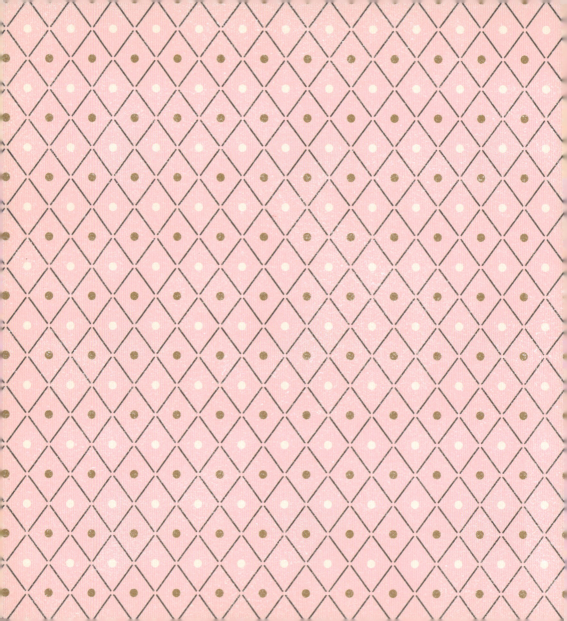

When I need
MY SISTER,
NO MATTER WHEN OR WHY,
YOU CAN ALWAYS
COUNT
ON HER TO BE RIGHT THERE.

SHE'S GOT A SENSE OF HUMOR

AND KNOWS HOW T

...MAKE ME LAUGH WITH HER OWN UNIQUE PERSPECTIVE ON THE WORLD.

She's FEISTY AND she's FIERCE, A FORCE THAT KNOWS NO STOPPING.

PATIENCE

IS HER SPECIALTY—

And she's got gentle
TOUGH-LOVE
when it comes to
real-life
TRUTHS.

I TRUST THE
WISDOM
THAT HER
HEART
WILL BRING.

When I'm in a
TIGHT SPOT
and I don't know who to
TURN TO,
my sister is the one who's
ALWAYS THERE.

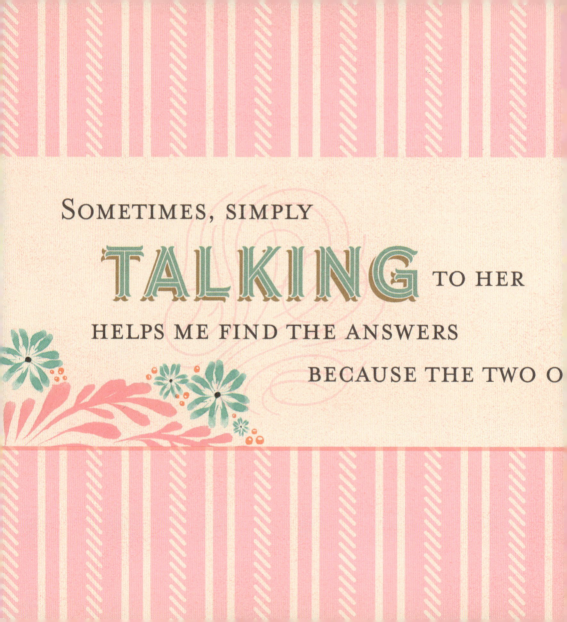

She's endlessly
SUPPORTIVE—

She wants what's
BEST
for others,
and I know she always
wants what's
BEST
for me.

That's why she'll
STAND
BEHIND ME,
OR EVEN RIGHT
BESIDE ME,
so I can do the things
I want to and succeed.

She always carries **KINDNESS** full o

She's
SMART
AND SHE'S
RESOURCEFUL,
CLEVER
AND
INSIGHTFUL,
AND ALWAYS GLAD TO SHARE
THE THINGS SHE KNOWS.

SHE LEARNS AND HOLDS
HER HEAD UP,
AND
FORGIVES
HERSELF WITH
LOVE
ALONG THE WAY.

And that's how she
REMINDS
me to be
GENTLE
with myself . . .

BECAUSE WE ALL
LEARN LESSONS
EVERY DAY.

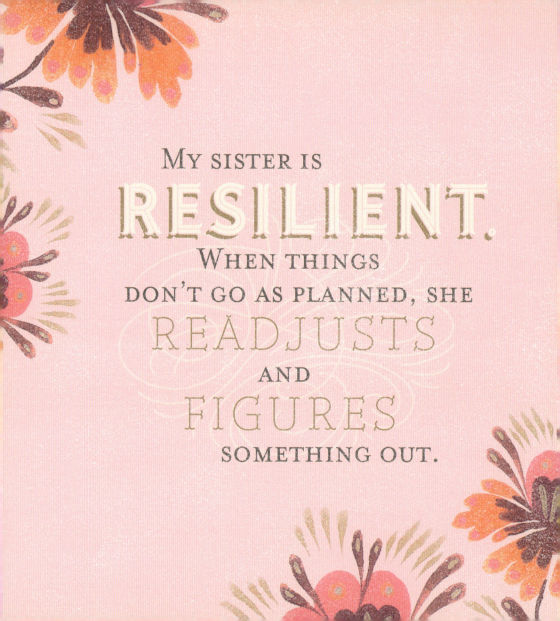

She knows that CHANGES happen and that being FLEXIBLE and POSITIVE is what life's all about.

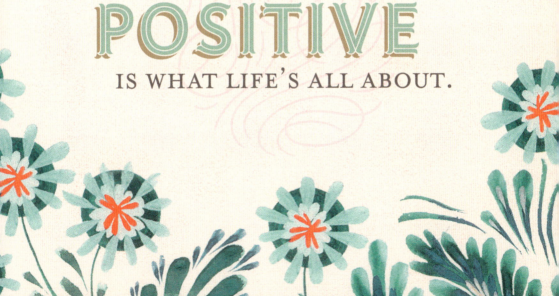

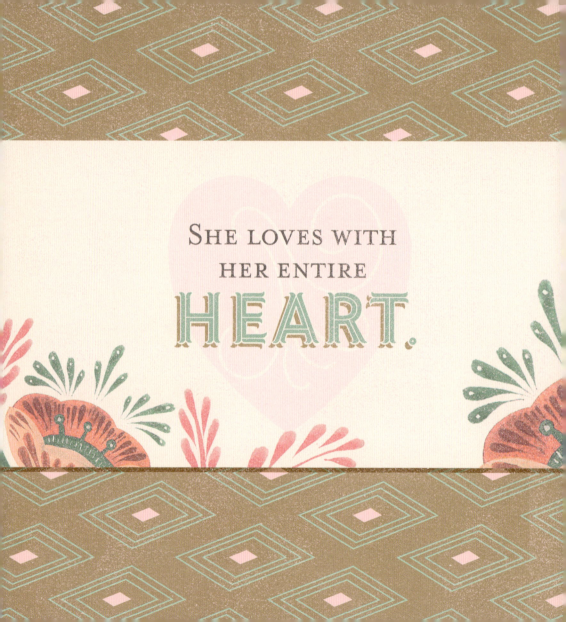

SHE LOVES WITH HER ENTIRE HEART.

Her hugs are
GENUINE
and she always has one ready
when I need it.

SHE UNDERSTANDS
MY FEELINGS
AND MY NAGGING NEED FOR
BROWNIES—

AND THAT WHEN YOU
HAVE A CRAVING,
YOU SHOULD FEED IT.

She's the "HOSTESS WITH

"THE MOST-ESS,"
AND WHEN WE'RE TOGETHER, HE MAKES ME FEEL RELAXED AND WANT TO STAY.

Her home's a
HAPPY HAVEN
from life's stresses and frustrations, and I'm
WELCOME
to come over any day.

SHE KNOWS ALL OF
MY STORIES–

EVEN THE MOST
EMBARRASSING.

BUT I KNOW THAT SHE
WILL NEVER TELL
A SOUL . . . RIGHT?

Her contagious positivity
SHINES BRIGHTLY
in her smile.

Life's challenges don't seem to TAKE A TOLL.

OMBINATION,
BECAUSE IF ANYONE HAS
GGING RIGHTS,
IT'S HER.

But she's very UNASSUMING about all that she's ACCOMPLISHED. She's a force for GOODNESS in the world.

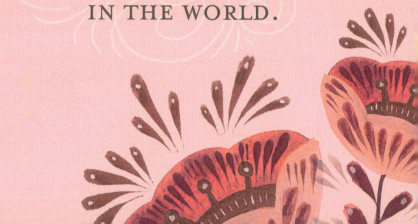

When I can't
MAKE MY
MIND UP
about which
clothes to buy,
I send her a text
and she
HELPS
ME DECIDE.

And don't forget
HOW MANY TIMES
we've cracked each other up
and made each other
LAUGH
until we cried.

She's always

INFLUENCED

me in more ways than I can count—

Yet she values my
UNIQUENESS
AND MY ONE-OF-A-KIND
SPIRIT.

I APPRECIATE
HER
MORE THAN
I CAN SAY.

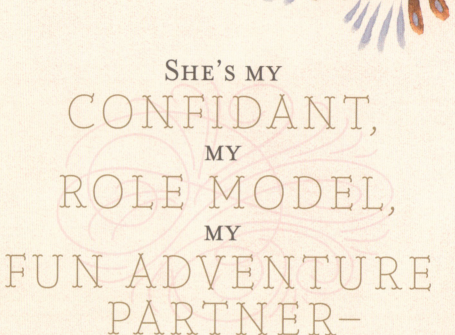

She's my
CONFIDANT,
MY
ROLE MODEL,
MY
FUN ADVENTURE
PARTNER–

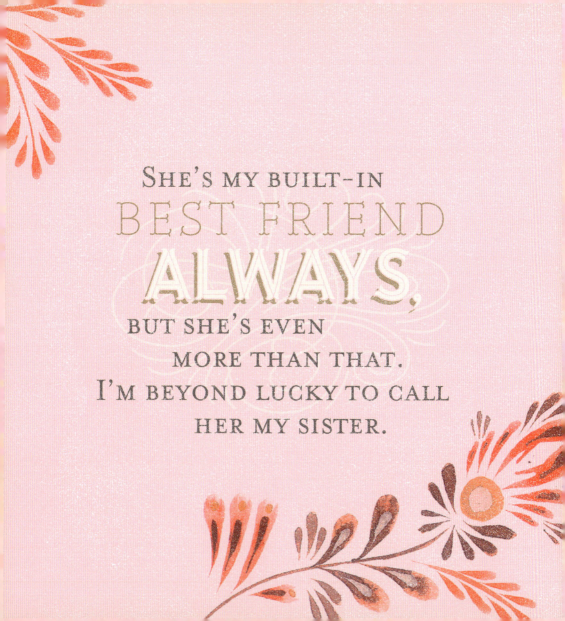

If you enjoyed this book
or it has touched your life in some way,
we'd love to hear from you.

Please write a review at Hallmark.com,
e-mail us at booknotes@hallmark.com,
or send your comments to:

Hallmark Book Feedback
P.O. Box 419034
Mail Drop 100
Kansas City, MO 64141